I0530627

THE CANCER YEARS:

SO FAR

ROLAND T WOODWARD

Copyrights © 2024 By

Roland T Woodward

All rights reserved. No part of this book may be reproduced or transmitted in any form by any means, electronic or mechanical, including photocopying and recording, or by any information storage and retrieval system, except as may be expressly permitted in writing from the author.

DEDICATION

This collection is dedicated to my partner and all the family who

shoulder the emotional heavy lifting of supporting me in my battle

with great strength, kindness and love.

ABOUT THE AUTHOR

Roland Woodward is a retired chartered forensic psychologist. He is dyslexic, which he regards as an enhancement. Living in the United Kingdom he has written poetry all his life and has now found time to join other poets in his local area and to consider publishing. This first short collection has been prompted by his battle with prostate cancer. Since being diagnosed in 2019 he has posted a regular blog for family and friends following the course of a life living with the disease in all its mundanity, crises and challenges. He hopes that there are more poetry collections will follow this small collection and that you find something of worth in this selection and those that may follow.

ACKNOWLEDGMENT

I extend my heartfelt gratitude to WritersClique.com for publishing this book, and a special thanks to Ted and Adam, my project managers, for their invaluable guidance. My editors, Anne and Shailene, deserve immense appreciation for their meticulous work and dedication. This book is a testament to the collective effort and talent of all involved.

TABLE OF CONTENTS

335

I know why old men stare,

Why they sit and look

 Nothing now is real

So we cling like Harlow's monkeys

 To the Terry towelling comfort of memory.

 All those moments when alive

When love, passion and life

Grabbed us and gave us meaning.

Now we see the world,

The bird on the wire,

The crow on the roof,

The raptor high in the sky,

We feel the air, the effort to fly.

None of what we are is here.

But the world remains,

It persists and so we watch,

We see the world.

And so we stare at it,

But it no longer gives us meaning,

We are in it,

But we are not of it.

June 2020

THE SHED.

336

Dumb with rage

I need to stop

Too much at Home

Needs seeing to.

Almost overwhelming

My teeth grind,

My gear low,

But always forward

I'm back.

Back in the Chinese box,

Normally I write,

I write a way out

But I am dumb

Of mouth and hand

So sit and calm

The inner Dark.

It is here,

My strength,

My gems,

The Anvil of My Forefathers.

The ironwork

of being.

20TH April 2022.

339

Like sitting by the pool

No sun

No waves

No laughing children

Or ice cream cones.

This is Windermere

Twinned with Sparta

As its babies die

On wooded hill sides

in the depths of June.

This is COVID meets BREXIT

This is empire alone,

A commonwealth of cold.

This where I sit

Balconied and overlooking

The memories of sun

And welcome on the continent,

 Now, the fog of Englishness

Cuts us off

But still, the bulldog

Gums its defiance

At bears, it used to bait.

This is where, in my woolly,

 I make my stand.

5-06-2022

THE LAKES, WINDERMERE

340

I am alone in my garden

Sun on my back

the air still.

This is my last day

No more employment,

Being useful,

making a difference.

Today, I stop being,

A forensic psychologist,

Professional,

expert.

I am alone in my garden

with days to fill,

a brain to feed

and all the fears

that stopping brings.

There is no me out there,

 no place in this world,

 so this is it.

I am alone in my garden

somehow, the words are sticky,

the ink blotchy

the flow difficult.

There are ghosts in my garden

and fears budding,

 flowers going over.

A noisy neighbour's mower.

I am alone in my garden.

16/June/2022

341

NATURE 1

Oh woe, where is my hedgehog

Two nights, the meaty bowl untouched

Two days, the garden camera blank.

Like a restaurateur, I miss my regular.

I pine and post photos on my blog,

I've close encountered but never clutched

To be familiar would be irregular.

Oh woe, I miss my trusty hog.

05/09/2022

342

NATURE **2**

Decisive, cold with rugged persistence,

Chrysanthemums to cancer

To nature, there is no resistance.

 No matter what the beauty

Or pangs and pains of plaque

Invites to tea are out of duty.

 Nature's nature cannot be trusted

It's bounty and favour inconsistent,

 Some would say maladjusted.

So, away with you natural force

I want no gamble in your game,

 In fact, I want divorce.

05/09/2022

343

NATURE 3

Fuck you Nature

You gave me Cancer

And now you want poems.

 Fuck you.

05/09/2022

344

I am one of life's accompanists,

 a pianist to a singer,

a backing vocalist to another.

 All my life, I've echoed,

I've reflected the art around me,

embellished, encouraged and applauded.

 All that is my own is sunk,

 mired in a talentless shell

that cannot be broken through.

It is a tragedy to know this

And yet persevere.

Grasping at thin air

the hope is to catch that moment

that others feel, recognise,

yet could not find the words for.

To communicate before knowing

what meaning it might contain.

 Finding the moment in this

second-hand world that lives

for that one sparkling

coming into the light.

03-10-2022

345

PROJECT DEATH.

Words from the grave,

a last, last word.

Neat packages of digital farewells,

all the things not said,

the reassurance that promises are kept,

the secrets now entombed,

dumb confessions confined forever.

It is a sort of honourable end.

Knowing these messages are heard,

delivered and then disposed of.

Only the going can be relied upon

there is no guarantee of coming to

at the time of ritual.

So quietly, I make my last declarations

of love, care and gratitude.

A chance to plug me in,

watch and listen,

finally, to press delete

and move on.

03-10-2022

346

They call my poetry

Bony.

No flesh

No story.

I open my eyes

There is light

And wonder,

this is enough.

18-09-2022

348

I break my rules,

Alone.

I subvert my plans,

Alone.

I sabotage the aim,

Alone.

And alone, I pay.

I flush,

All I want to do

is take my clothes off.

It's that simple,

fighting beyond the losses,

don't expect me to be

nice about it.

10-11-2022

HOLIDAY INN YORK.

349

I can't write,

I'm uninspired,

It's the cold,

the sleet

that hangs around

my heart.

Somehow, I am not working,

frozen and iced up.

The world holds no interest,

no flow or inspiration.

So, this is winter

Snowed in and

Snowed under.

When I lose my poetry

I've lost engagement,

I no longer notice,

I'm emotionally immobile.

It is a little death,

the other end of orgasm.

Around me, the world is 2D

And reality is debatable,

Nothing tugs, knocks, impinges,

I'm hard-wrapped in a shell.

Inside are unmet needs

that dare not say their names,

and the Dark and Tricky

ripples ominously, whispering,

"You are mine."

Gone are the days

When a brandy and a decent shag

would see the world right.

This is what being at war

with Cancer in your balls

does to you.

Fuck Cancer!

I should be so lucky.

12-12-20

COSY CAFÉ HINCKLEY.

350

As I press one foot

After another

In the gym

I sense the rhythm

That took me,

Marathoned me

And told me

You're alive.

I reach for that feeling

Like a lover's arms around me,

I need salvation

As I fight

To stay alive.

I stride on

Rammstein loud in my ears

Halfisch

Halfisch

Driving me

Perpetually moving

To stay alive,

I am afraid in this struggle.

Halfisch

Halfisch

Halfisch

In der tiefe es einsam

In the deep it is lonely

So die tranen sieht man nicht

So no one can see the tears.

20-12-2022

SHED.

351

What do I do?

I write,

I garden

I clean the house.

Something missing?

Like an alcoholic

with no kidneys,

a diver

without lungs.

It's just a construction,

Impressions synapsed together

in a process

welded with transmitters

cell by cell.

On or off,

It either is or isn't

Like life,

You either are or aren't.

Costa Hinkley 10-01-2023

(59 words)

352

All I ever was

was a wordsmith.

Dyslexic silver tongue

who knew the shapes

and colours of symbols.

Always trying to tell others

this is how it is for me.

It aroused no interest

so I go on

seeking that moment

that says clearly

this is me.

That instance

when another's eyes light

and there are two of us.

Same place

Same time

Same understanding.

Hinkley 10-01-2023

(70 words)

353

My radio

All knobs and dials

FM loud and proud

Blasts out

and blastomas.

It's slaying a tumour

It's wild and a rumour

that pill and potion

 kick up a commotion.

Rock and rollology

Biology and physiology

Burn, scar and cullology

On my radiology.

So go, man go

And scorch away,

Tomorrows so

a hot day.

Old and gay,

I could spit

This cutting ray

Drill bit

Sunk within

My skin,

Is no mix,

ain't no fix.

354

Settle down; you've seen a pensioner in a suit before.

Maybe not vertical,

more wood encased on a rainy afternoon

with a lot of people looking into a hole

and wishing it was all over.

Except that, no matter how hard you try,

you cannot help thinking,

"Did he leave me anything? Am I in the will?"

I'm just getting my monies worth out of mine

before an unsuspecting stranger grabs it

as a bargain from Sod the Aged.

I hate old people,

Why cannot they all die tragically young?

Why do they hang on till everyone is guilt-ridden?

Thinking it would be a relief when they go?

Yes, yes, a couple of you love Nanna

but what a pain she is.

How many times has she buried

her teeth in the garden?

REWORKED FROM 2019

26-03-2023

355

(Instruction for reading: Add your own commas and full stops. Only comas and full stops; everything else is too fancy. You may use 1 octave, or two quatrains to make up the first stanza and the remaining sestet for the final stanza.)

Too sore for Peaky Blinders, a traditional English sonnet

Fuck fuck fuck fuck fuck fuck fuck fuck fuck fuck

Fuck fuck fuck fuck fuck fuck fuck fuck fuck fuck

Fuck fuck fuck fuck fuck fuck fuck fuck fuck fuck

Fuck fuck fuck fuck fuck fuck fuck fuck fuck fuck

Fuck fuck fuck fuck fuck fuck fuck fuck fuck fuck

Fuck fuck fuck fuck fuck fuck fuck fuck fuck fuck

Fuck fuck fuck fuck fuck fuck fuck fuck fuck fuck

Fuck fuck fuck fuck fuck fuck fuck fuck fuck fuck

Fuck fuck fuck fuck fuck fuck fuck fuck fuck fuck

Fuck fuck fuck fuck fuck fuck fuck fuck fuck fuck

Fuck fuck fuck fuck fuck fuck fuck fuck fuck fuck

Fuck fuck fuck fuck fuck fuck fuck fuck fuck fuck

Fuck fuck fuck fuck fuck fuck fuck fuck fuck fuck

Fuck fuck fuck fuck fuck fuck fuck fuck Cancer.

27-05-2023

356

I quit!

Says it all.

I resign

From everything.

No more

Of anything.

No effort

for no act.

I'm done,

dusted down

to a skeleton,

and then the fucker

interrupts with painkillers.

What's in it for me?

Peaceful death

is apparently not

an option.

So,

Grind

Grind

On

and

On.

10 May 2023

357

The pyre burns,

Words to ashes

and I grieve,

left with the

imprescriptibility

of experience.

11-07-2023

359

Twenty-three and a half

By twenty-three and a half inches.

A measuring tape.

Two laptops and stands

With mouse and mat, top layer.

Down.

Used envelop, deceased RAC card,

Hard drives, external.

Hair band, rubber band, box cutter,

Ear buds, biro, gimlet.

USB stick, glasses, glasses reading,

Bulldog clip, paper clip, expended paracetamol.

Paper note, post office receipt, postage stamps.

Sticky note flags, silver ring box,

Remote and coffee glass;

Almost overlooked the fifty pence pieces, rare.

This is the archaeology of a dying life,

Or, another instillation by Tracey.

03-08-2023 @ 10:30

After Tracey Emine. Guide price £50,000.

If you think £50,000 is a joke, remember Tracey Emin's bed installation went for £2,400,000, purportedly representing her struggle with a period of severe emotional flux, so I reckon that wrestling with stage 4 cancer got to be worth at least £50,000. You see how absurd the world is and must not be taken seriously.

360

This sheet is waiting

like a conductor's baton.

The hand that holds the pen,

frozen in icy lock.

Surrounded by painted glass,

half-finished quarter boards,

scribbled notes for books,

friend's art and wax;

the jewellery yet to be caste.

But at this moment,

Nothing, a desert of blankness.

So, this page waits

like an act of faith,

and equally illogical.

The wall is a question,

Who do I trust enough

To be the executor of my Will.

I know the nooks and crannies

of people too well

to assume that death

cleans the soul

and makes others honest,

unbendable and true.

A puppet for the hand

of death.

9TH August 2023

361

It's time.

Time to say farewell,

bite the bullet and concede to the scythe.

Like the inevitability

Of harvest,

I yield.

Carefully, I select

the items

and, with them, the memories.

With each comes stitched-in

reminiscences.

Each pair are transitional items

that will be jettisoned,

recycled or forgotten.

Reality confrontation

at a brutal level.

A mirror that won't be denied

And is now avoided.

I'm never going to be the same

and gone is the possibility.

I am beyond any clever fix

My waistline will never again be 36.

13-08-2023

362

Forged in Worker Association concerts,

random tickets for loggia, box or stall,

or museum trips,

I learnt culture.

Aspiring working class

exposing children to better things.

There were rules;

No debt,

work hard,

achieve at education,

be socialist, liberal and tolerant.

Go on marches, ban the bomb,

and avoid South African goods.

Segregation is bad,

fairness and equality are the way.

Be a good co-op member,

look after family and neighbours,

we are in this shit together.

My mother, a life- long Labour member,

died a racist, swamped

by all the fruits of her efforts.

A community she no longer recognised,

surrounded by tongues she did not speak,

beholden to people she had fought for.

She did not understand how being white

put her out of being right.

Told to feel the guilt of privilege,

told her life of struggle

or family and friends

was all wrong.

Of how she was ignorant,

uninformed and disposable.

Even before we got woke

she craved release,

it had all become too much,

her world had turned.

Now dying, her son

feels the underachieving

white teenager rage again.

The drudgery today boys

and the still told, "your

not good enough" youth.

Everything here is not for you,

Ignorance is yours,

Fault is yours,

and the community wonders why

there is resentment when the message is,

The future is not for you,

There's no place for you.

So suck it up, worker boy

We don't give a fuck

That's the way it is

Init.

So, it circles

Generation on generation

Without concerts or conscience,

Art or consideration.

There will be a backlash,

blacklash and barbarity

and a new era darker than before.

This sceptred isle,

This blessed plot, this earth, this realm,

This England

Hath made a shameful

Conquest of itself.

Fucked init.

13-08-2023.

www.ingramcontent.com/pod-product-compliance
Lightning Source LLC
Chambersburg PA
CBHW070945120626
46546CB00004B/1572